New Friends in a New Land

A Thanksgiving Story

by Judith Bauer Stamper

Alex Haley, General Editor

Illustrations by Chet Jezierski

RSVP

RAINTREE
STECK-VAUGHN
PUBLISHERS
The Steck-Vaughn Company

Austin, Texas

To Genevieve, with thanks

Published by Steck-Vaughn Company.

Cover art by Chet Jezierski

Printed in the United States of America
  2 3 4 5 6 7 8 9 R 98 97 96 95 94 93

Library of Congress Cataloging-in-Publication Data

Stamper, Judith Bauer.
    New friends in a new land: a Thanksgiving story/Judith Bauer Stamper; illustrator, Chet Jezierski.
        p.   cm.—(Stories of America)
    Summary: Describes the Pilgrims' first year in Plymouth and the first Thanksgiving.
    ISBN 0-8114-7213-2.—ISBN 0-8114-8053-4 (softcover)
    1. Pilgrims (New Plymouth Colony)—Juvenile literature. 2. Massachusetts—History—New Plymouth, 1620–1691—Juvenile literature. 3. Thanksgiving Day—Juvenile literature. [1. Pilgrims (New Plymouth Colony) 2. Massachusetts—History—New Plymouth, 1620–1691. 3. Thanksgiving Day.]
I. Jezierski, Chet, ill.   II. Title.   III. Series.
F68.S776   1993
974.4'8202—dc20

                                                                                                    92-18072
                                                                                                    CIP
                                                                                                    AC

ISBN 0-8114-7213-2 (Hardcover)
ISBN 0-8114-8053-4 (Softcover)

A Note
from Alex Haley, General Editor

Before people are friends or enemies, they are strangers. They don't know each other. They have only just met. They might look a little different to one another. Their way of doing things might be a little different. Having met, they must decide: friends or enemies?

How this question is answered is the story of *New Friends in a New Land*. It is a Thanksgiving story with a lesson for us all. You are always thankful for your friends, but never for your enemies. Choose friendship.

Damaris Hopkins sat on her father's knee in front of the kitchen fire. Beside her, Mrs. Hopkins held baby Oceanus. Her brother Giles and sister Constance sat nearby.

It was the year 1621. Just a few months ago, Damaris had come to America from England. She and her family had sailed on the ship called the *Mayflower*. Now they lived in a village named Plymouth.

Damaris looked into the fire and wished for the hundredth time that winter was over. She knew that food was running short. People were dying of sickness. And everyone worried about the Indians. The Indians had lived on the land around Plymouth first. What would happen if they wanted their land back?

Damaris shivered and drew closer to her father. Her father hugged her and her mother gave her a smile. Damaris smiled bravely back.

A few days later, Damaris woke up early and pushed open the front door. The sun was just coming up over the rooftops.

Damaris sniffed the air. Something was different about it. It smelled like spring!

Damaris ran inside and shouted that spring was here. Oceanus started to cry, but the rest of the family laughed.

After her morning chores, Damaris ran outside to watch Father and Giles. They were adding thatch to the roof.

Just then, Damaris looked down the street. She could hardly believe her eyes!

10

A tall Indian was walking into Plymouth. "Welcome, Englishmen," he said.

Damaris hid behind a fence and watched him. He carried a bow and two arrows. His black hair hung long in back.

The Indian called himself Samoset. He had learned some English from explorers. He was eager to talk to the Pilgrims. And they had many questions to ask him. The Pilgrims were glad that Samoset could talk to them in English.

Samoset told them about the land where Plymouth was built. The Patuxet Indians had cleared it. But they had all died of a great sickness. After that no other Indians wanted the land.

The Pilgrims were glad to have Samoset as a friend. They gave him cheese, biscuits, and duck to eat. And they gave him a coat to wear.

Damaris watched Samoset all day. He seemed friendly. But Damaris knew almost nothing about Indians. She felt a little afraid but curious at the same time.

The sun began to set in the sky. Mrs. Hopkins came running in to tell the children the news. She said Samoset was spending the night in their house!

The tall Indian walked through the door. Damaris did not know what to expect. She hid in the shadows and stared. Samoset saw her hiding and smiled.

Mrs. Hopkins gave Samoset a rug to sleep on. Samoset wrapped it around his body. Soon, he was sound asleep.

But Damaris did not go to sleep for a long time.

The next day Samoset prepared to leave. He promised to come back to Plymouth again. And he kept his word. A short time later, he came back with a man named Squanto.

Squanto spoke English very well. At one time, he had been kidnapped and taken to England by ship.

Damaris listened to Squanto's story with surprise. The English had done him a great wrong. Yet he still wanted to be their friend.

That same day, a great chief named Massasoit came to Plymouth with sixty Wampanoag Indians. Massasoit's face was painted a dark red. He wore a deerskin over one shoulder and white bone beads around his neck.

18

The Pilgrims put out a great welcome. They played the trumpet and drums. They gave Massasoit food and drink. Squanto helped the Pilgrims talk with the Wampanoags. By the end of the day, they signed a treaty. They promised to live as friends in peace.

19

After that, Damaris stopped being afraid of the Indians. She even became good friends with Squanto. He showed Damaris how to play an Indian game called hubbub. Damaris got so good at it that she could beat Squanto.

Squanto stayed in Plymouth all that spring and summer. He showed the Pilgrims how to dig for clams in the mud by the bay.

He showed them how to plant corn seeds
with dead fish to make the plants grow. And
he knew which wild berries were good to eat.

Soon, the days grew shorter and colder. Damaris kept busy helping store food for the winter. She picked ears of corn from the fields. She helped salt codfish for winter meals. And she laid out fruit to dry in the late summer sun.

The Pilgrims knew it was time to give thanks to God and their Indian friends. They decided to have a harvest feast. Everyone worked to get ready.

Mr. Hopkins went out hunting. He came back with ducks, geese, and turkey. Mrs. Hopkins baked corn bread and cooked a big pot of fish soup.

Damaris picked herbs from the kitchen garden. She added wood to the cooking fires. And she begged Squanto to bring some Indian children to the feast.

On the big day, Massasoit walked into Plymouth with ninety men. The Pilgrims knew there would never be enough food to go around.

Massasoit fixed the problem by sending his men out hunting. They came back with five deer to roast over the open fire.

Before sitting down to eat, the Pilgrims and the Wampanoags gave thanks. Then they began the feast. Damaris ate until her stomach hurt.

The feast went on and on for three days.
Damaris played tug-of-war and pillow pushing
with the other Pilgrim children. She watched
the Wampanoags dance and sing.

Best of all, she saw a Wampanoag girl who was about her own age. The girl was playing hubbub with her brother. Damaris went up to watch. Soon, she was playing with them.

At sunset on the third day, the Wampanoags went home. Damaris waved good-bye as they walked into the woods. Her new friend turned and waved back.

That night Damaris fell into bed, tired and happy. It had been a wonderful time of thanksgiving.

Like Damaris, we give thanks each year. On Thanksgiving Day, we join our families and friends for prayer, feasting, and fun.

We remember the Pilgrims who started a new life in America. We remember the Indians who helped them. And we remember children like Damaris who worked and played at the first Thanksgiving.

31

Thanksgiving Day

Thanksgiving Day is one of our national holidays. It is celebrated on the fourth Thursday of November. During this holiday we spend time with friends and family.

Even before 1621, the Spanish and English settlers had their own thanksgiving celebrations. Squanto's people also celebrated a thanksgiving holiday. Each was different, but each was a way of giving thanks for family, for food, and for life.

In 1863 President Abraham Lincoln made Thanksgiving Day a national holiday. He knew that it was important to celebrate the good in life, even during difficult times.

Today, more than ever, Thanksgiving Day is an important day to celebrate. It is a special time that you can share with your family, with your friends, and with all the people of the world.

DATE DUE
